SOMEWHERE BETTER

Written by
Leonard Mendoza

Illustrated by
Bonnie Lemaire

Halo
PUBLISHING
INTERNATIONAL

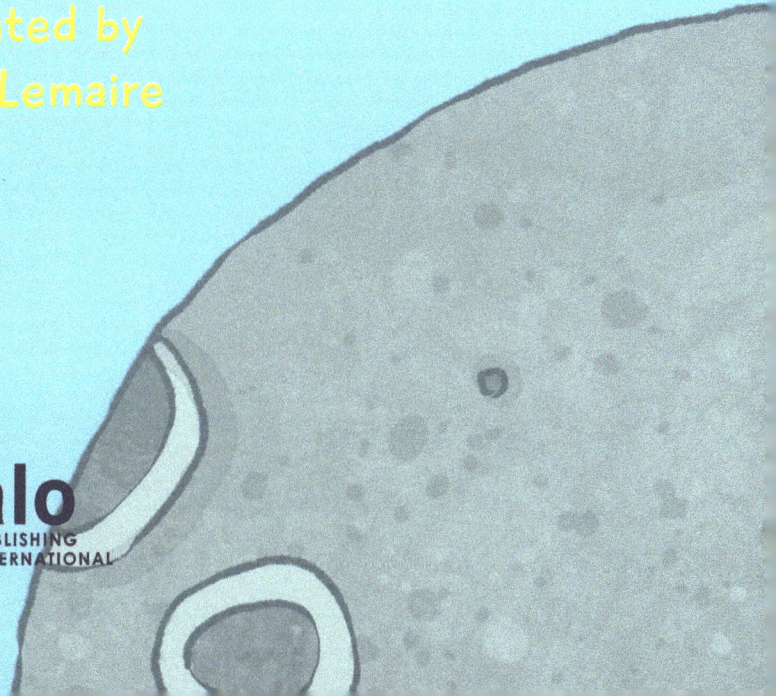

ISBN: 978-1-63765-248-0
LCCN: 2022909620

Halo
PUBLISHING
INTERNATIONAL

Halo Publishing International, LLC
www.halopublishing.com

Printed and bound in the United States of America

To my mom, Josie,
my biggest supporter.

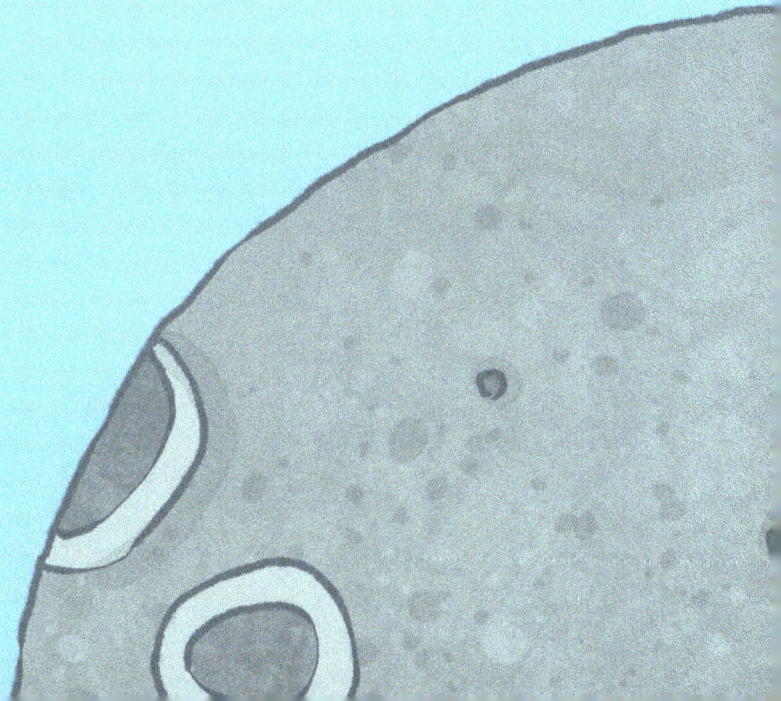

Billy is a boy who loves to play, more than anything. He plays with his friends every single day. One day, Billy got bored of doing the same things and playing the same games over and over again. So Billy decided he was going to build a rocket ship! There was no better place he could imagine playing than on the Moon. At last, Billy would play somewhere that no one had ever played before.

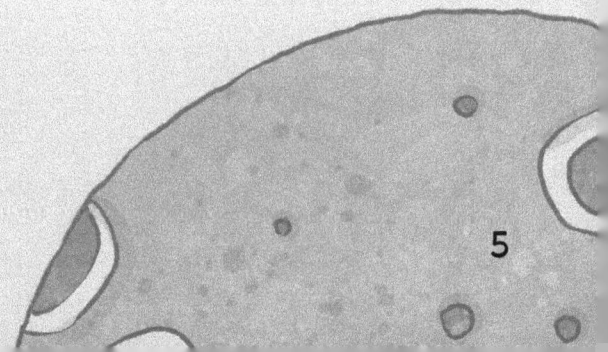

Suddenly, two of Billy's friends came along to see if Billy wanted to play. Tex and Lexi are brother and sister, and also Billy's neighbors. "Hey, Billy! Want to come over to our house and jump on the trampoline with us? Or maybe play on the swings?"

"No way! I'm going to take a trampoline and a set of swings to the Moon. Then I'll be able to jump and swing higher than anyone ever has before!" Billy exclaimed.

Saddened, Tex and Lexi began to walk back to their home.

Just as Billy was getting back to work, two more of his friends came over filled with energy and eager to play with Billy. Ruth and Ralphie are neighbors who live at the end of the street. Excited to see him, Ruth shouted, "Hey, Billy! Hope you're ready to play with us, because we're gonna race each other and play hide-and-seek!"

Billy scoffed and said, "Thanks, but no thanks! I don't have time to waste, and I will need all of my strength to build the rocket."

"We understand," said Ralphie. But he and Ruth still felt down after Billy's refusal to play with them.

9

Then along came Shawn, Billy's best friend who lives across the street. Shawn and Billy do almost everything together, and Billy can always count on Shawn for anything.

Billy turned, noticed Shawn, and then said, "Oh, hey, Shawn! Come in! I'm building a rocket ship to go to the Moon so I can play and be the happiest person ever!"

"What's wrong with playing here on Earth? With your toys and friends here, don't you have everything you need? Don't they make you happy enough?"

Billy frowned and said, "No! I want more! I need more, and I won't be happy until I go to the Moon!"

Shawn began to walk away, but then he turned and said, "Don't lose yourself while trying to get to the top; happiness is right where you are."

Shawn's words buzzed around inside Billy's head with confusion. But he had no time to waste; he needed to create his control desk somehow. He needed buttons, levers, and a steering wheel, but where would he find anything like that?

He looked around and couldn't help but notice how all the toys in his toy box looked just the right size for his control desk. "Yes! My toy blocks will be my buttons, and my toy swords will be my levers, and my bicycle handles will be my steering wheel!"

After that, Billy ran into another problem. How was he going to cover the rocket and make walls for it? "This one is going to be tough to figure out," said Billy as he walked to his clubhouse.

Billy really loved his clubhouse and remembering all the fun times he'd had in there as he was growing up. He would often use it as a place to go and think. Or if he was ever feeling sad, being in the clubhouse would make him happy again.

As Billy sat there and tried to figure out how he was going to cover his rocket, he couldn't help but notice...the walls in his clubhouse would be perfect to use for the rocket.

CLUB HOUSE

"I'm almost done! All I need now is to find a helmet that I can wear in outer space."

There was almost nothing Billy had that could be used as a helmet. Then he looked over to his fish swimming around in the nice, big fishbowl. He'd named his fish Plum because he was purple and almost looked like a plum. And Billy couldn't help but notice...his fishbowl would fit perfectly over his head. So he took Plum out of the bowl and put him in a glass jar.

"Oh boy! Now is the time! I have everything I need, and I'm ready to take off!" Billy said excitedly. Without another word, Billy went inside his ship to get ready to go straight to the Moon. "All systems ready! Time for blastoff!" shouted Billy as he flipped the switch.

The ship began to shake and rumble. Suddenly, Billy noticed clouds passing by the window. Then the ship began to shake even more and made a lot of noise. All of a sudden, the shaking stopped, and everything was very calm.

Billy looked out the window and saw that he was already in space and headed towards the Moon. He kept his eyes on the Moon the whole time; the nearer Billy got to it, the more his excitement grew.

Finally, it was time to prepare for landing. After successfully touching down on the Moon's surface, Billy carefully ventured out of the rocket ship. He began to feel excitement with every step he took.

To the moon...

So as he said he would, Billy took out his trampoline and swings, and he set them up on the surface of the Moon. He jumped on his trampoline, but in the Moon's atmosphere, it took so long just to come back down to the trampoline that he got bored. Billy climbed off the trampoline and got on his swings, but he just floated and couldn't do anything because of the Moon's weak gravity. There was no way he could race or play hide-and-seek because there was nobody with whom to race or play.

Billy turned around, looked at the Earth, and began to miss all of his friends. Suddenly, Shawn's words began to make sense to Billy. *"Happiness is right where you are."* Billy was definitely not happy, and he said, "I gave a lot just to get here, but I've lost the things that I love most."

Billy took apart his trampoline and swings and carried them back to the rocket ship. Then he flipped the switch on the control desk and headed back to Earth.

As Billy was landing, he noticed that all of his friends were there on the ground. Right when he stepped out, they all came and gave him a big group hug.

"We've missed you so much!" said Ralphie.

"I was very worried about you!" said Tex.

Billy said, "Really? I didn't know you all would still like me after I turned you all down. But I still came back because I missed you all so much."

"Of course, we care! Why wouldn't we?" said Ruth.

"You're our friend; we at least have to make sure you're safe!" said Lexi.

Shawn came over, gave Billy a big hug, and said, "The people who love you will always be here for you, no matter what."

"Wow," said Billy, "I feel so lucky to have people who love me so much and still accept me. There is definitely no better place than right here."

www.ingramcontent.com/pod-product-compliance
Lightning Source LLC
LaVergne TN
LVHW070839080426
835511LV00025B/3484